SONGS
FOR THE
LAST SUNRISE

Poems And Prayers From The Edge Of Eternity

TOD TRUETTNER

SONGS

FOR THE

LAST SUNRISE

Poems And Prayers From The Edge Of Eternity

TOD TRUETTNER

ARPress
ILLUMINATING IDEAS.
EMPOWERING VOICES

ARPress
45 Dan Road Suite 15
Canton MA 02021
  Hotline: 1(888) 821-0229
  Fax: 1(508) 545-7580

Ordering Information:
Quantity sales. Special discounts are available on quantity purchases by corporations, associations, and others. For details, contact the publisher at the address above.

Printed in the United States of America.

ISBN-13:   Softcover   979-8-89676-685-8
             eBook   979-8-89676-686-5

Library of Congress Control Number: 2025924884

Dedication

For every soul that has wrestled with faith, feared the silence, or stood
in the fire—
this book is for you.

And to my family, whose love holds me up,
and to the Lord, who never let me go—
this is your story too.

For the ones who held on when the light grew dim.
For those still watching, still believing,
still singing in the dark.

And for my family—on earth and in heaven—
who taught me that love stands guard through the night
and rises with the dawn.

Part I

Let It Be So

Poetic Prayers from the Heart of a Builder

Foreword

This book was never meant to be just poems or prayers.
It was born from sweat, sorrow, and sacred moments—some
whispered, some screamed.
It came to life while I was still learning how to live.

I am a builder by trade. I work with steel and wood, shaping what can
be seen and held.
But somewhere along the way, God began shaping something in me.
Through illness, through loss, through quiet nights of questioning and
mornings filled with grace—I began to see that faith isn't built only in
the pews.
It's built in the pain, in the labor, in the silence... and sometimes in the
darkest places where we find we're still breathing.

This book is a reflection of my journey with God—not just the
victories, but the valleys.
It's a prayer for the soul that questions, the heart that struggles, and
the hands that keep building even when they're tired.
It's for anyone who's ever asked, "Is He still here?"
And for those who've heard the whisper in return: "Yes, child. I never
left."

You'll find pieces about doubt. About anger. About sacred work and
the Kingdom within.
You'll walk through the cry for awakening, the battle within, the holy
labor of life, and the eternal hope that holds us up.

Each poem is a prayer. Each prayer is a piece of the road I've walked.
And if you've walked through anything like it, then maybe these words
can be a companion to you.

Whether you're kneeling, building, resting, or rising...
Whether you're at the beginning or somewhere deep in the middle...
May you find the grace that has never stopped pursuing you.

Let this book remind you:
You are not forgotten.
You are not your past.
You are being built—day by day—by a God who sees every swing of the hammer and every beat of the heart.

So from one soul to another...
Welcome.
Let's walk this road together.

Let it be so.

— Tod Truettner

□ Part 1: Table of Content

The Cry for Awakening

When the soul begins to stir, to question, to reach...

There comes a moment when comfort cracks,
and a whisper rises beneath the noise.
This is the beginning of the turning—
the holy ache, the sacred unrest.
These prayers are for the ones who are just waking up.

Before the First Amen

A Poetic Prayer of Uncertain Faith

I don't know if I believe enough
To pray the way the others do—
With folded hands and perfect words,
And hearts that seem so sure of You.

But still, I feel You in the pause,
In breaths I didn't know were prayer—
In questions whispered late at night,
When no one else is really there.

I don't yet have the scripture worn,
Or language polished bright with use.
But something deeper stirs in me—
A hunger I cannot refuse.

So here I am, not kneeling bold,
Not raising arms or shouting loud—
Just standing in a quiet place,
No choir, no crowd, no sacred shroud.

Is this a prayer? I'm not quite sure.
But if You're there, then maybe—*yes.*
A heart turned slightly toward the light,
A soul too tired to second-guess.

If You are love, then meet me here.
Not at the altar—but the edge.
And catch me where the silence lives,
Before the first Amen is said.

Scripture Reference
Romans 8:26 (NIV)

"In the same way, the Spirit helps us in our weakness.
We do not know what we ought to pray for, but the Spirit himself intercedes for us
through wordless groans."

The Door You Keep Knocking On

A Poetic Prayer of Reluctant Surrender

There's a door I've kept closed for years,
With locks I forged from fear and pride.
Not because I hate the light—
But sometimes darkness feels like pride.

You knock, but not with angry fists.
You wait with patience, not with scorn.
You do not barge, You do not break—
You've knocked since long before I was born.

I've heard You in the quiet night,
The sudden stillness in my breath.
I've felt You near, though not yet seen—
A presence brushing past regret.

Why do You knock and knock again,
When I've ignored, dismissed, denied?
Why not move on to purer hearts,
To cleaner hands, to stronger lives?

But still You knock—soft, low, and sure,
As if You know the mess inside.
And yet, You long to enter still—
Not to condemn, but to abide.

So here I stand, the key in hand,
Unsure of what You'll find within.
But if You love me as You say,
Then come, and let the work begin.

I may not open wide just yet—
But inch by inch, I'll draw You near.
And if You knock again tonight,
I pray this time... I'll lose my fear.

Scripture Reference
Revelation 3:20 (NIV)

"Here I am! I stand at the door and knock.
If anyone hears my voice and opens the door,
I will come in and eat with that person, and they with me."

Wake Me Up Inside

A Poetic Prayer of Holy Reawakening

Wake me up, O Lord of light—
Not just from sleep, but from the haze.
Shake loose the dust upon my soul,
And set my heart again ablaze.

I've walked too long with eyes half-closed,
With dreams forgotten, faith gone dim.
But still I know—You formed my frame,
And placed Your glory deep within.

Not broken clay, not flawed design,
But crafted by a perfect hand—
You whispered purpose in my bones,
Before my feet could even stand.

So wake me up inside, O God—
Let fire rise where fear once reigned.
Unshutter every blinded eye,
Unchain the gifts that still remain.

Let me not waste the breath You give,
The voice You formed to speak Your name.
Unveil the strength I never knew,
The Spirit's power, the holy flame.

Remind me I was made for more
Than passing time or chasing praise—
I am Your child, Your flame, Your work,
Alive to burn with Heaven's blaze.

So stir the soul, awake the light,
And flood this heart with holy pride—
Not pride in self, but joy in You—
The One who woke me up inside.

Scripture Reference
Ephesians 5:14 (NIV)

"Wake up, sleeper, rise from the dead, and Christ will shine on you."

I Hear Your Voice

A Poetic Prayer in Quiet Faith

I asked the sky for answers clear,
For signs to blaze along the way—
For thundered truths, for parted seas,
For You to speak and not delay.

But silence sat beside my plea,
And I began to doubt Your will—
Until I heard, not shout or storm,
But whisper soft and still.

A gentle pull upon my heart,
A hush that sang behind the day—
A thought I hadn't placed myself,
A warning not to stray.

It wasn't loud—it never is—
No lightning strike, no flaming tree.
But just enough to turn my steps,
To guide the soul of me.

I heard Your voice in morning's hush,
In weeping winds and restless dreams—
In laughter shared, in quiet grief,
In life between the seams.

You spoke through pauses in my plans,
Through doors unopened, calls unmet—
Through every no I didn't want,
And every yes I don't regret.

Now when I ask, "Are You still near?"
And all the world gives back is gray,
I close my eyes, and there You are—
Still whispering the way.

So speak again, in wind or breath,
In ancient word or newborn choice—
However small, however soft,
Lord, let me hear Your voice.

Scripture Reference
1 Kings 19:11–12 (NIV)

*"The Lord was not in the wind... nor the earthquake... nor the fire...
But after the fire came a gentle whisper."*

Can Words Change the World?

A Poetic Prayer for a Culture in Chaos

Can words, once spoken, shape the air?
Can syllables rewrite the sky?
Do whispered thoughts, like seeds, take root—
And live long after lips go dry?

I've seen a phrase unkindly cast
Leave scars no medicine could mend.
I've heard the echo of a lie
Outlive the breath that let it bend.

But if words can break, then can they build?
If curses burn, can blessings bloom?
If voices carry hate like fire,
Can grace speak peace into a room?

O Lord, You shaped the stars with sound,
You spun the cosmos with a phrase—
And Christ, the Word, walked flesh and bone
To set our wandering hearts ablaze.

So teach me, Lord, to speak with care—
To guard the weight my words can wield.
To bind the broken with my voice,
To speak a truth that heals and shields.

Let not my mouth be sharpened steel,
Or poisoned well from which I draw.
Let kindness be the language learned,
Let love become the only law.

For in this world where noise is king,
And every screen becomes a stage—
Let those who follow You speak light,
And walk with wisdom, not with rage.

Yes, words can change the world, my God—
They always have, they always will.
So let me speak with holy fire,
But never flame that aims to kill.

Scripture Reference
Proverbs 18:21 (NIV)

*"The tongue has the power of life and death,
and those who love it will eat its fruit."*

The Question That Won't Let Me Go

A Poetic Prayer of Sacred Curiosity

There's a question buried deep in me—
It knocks, it hums, it won't let go.
It's not a doubt, it's not despair—
But something older than I know.

It rises when the world grows quiet,
When laughter fades and lights go dim.
It echoes in the in-between—
A voice I can't outrun or trim.

Is there more?—it softly asks.
More than comfort, more than gain?
A purpose shaped beyond the grave,
A joy not born from luck or pain?

I've chased success, I've built my name,
I've filled my life with crafted show—
But still, this question follows me—
The one that will not let me go.

Perhaps it is Your voice, O Lord,
Not thunder, but a gentle prod—
A whisper asking me to seek,
To leave the known and search for God.

So if You placed it there, this ache,
Then let it draw me to Your face—
And let the question lead me home,
By way of wonder, doubt, and grace.

Scripture Reference
Jeremiah 29:13 (NIV)

"You will seek me and find me when you seek me with all your heart."

Whispers in the Waiting

A Poetic Prayer for the In-Between

I asked You once for thunder, Lord,
For parting skies, for signs, for flame.
But all I heard was quiet wind,
And still… I whispered out Your name.

The waiting isn't absence, though—
It only feels like hollow space.
But somehow, in this silent stretch,
I sense the breath of hidden grace.

You're not delaying just to test,
Or watching from some distant height.
You're working where my eyes can't see,
And planting truth before it's light.

In waiting, pride begins to fade,
And roots grow deep in unseen soil.
You're shaping me for what will bloom—
Through patient peace, not frantic toil.

A whisper doesn't force its way,
It waits until the heart leans in.
And that is where I find You most—
Not loud, but loving, deep within.

So teach me how to wait with joy,
Not clenched with fear, but held in trust.
For You are not a God of clocks,
But of redemption, full and just.

I'll stay right here until You speak,
And if You never shout or show—
Then let me find You in the hush,
The God who whispers as I grow.

Scripture Reference
Lamentations 3:25–26 (NIV)

*"The Lord is good to those whose hope is in him, to the one who seeks him;
it is good to wait quietly for the salvation of the Lord."*

🗡 The Battle Within

Where doubt and darkness wrestle with light and grace...

Faith isn't always a banner—it's often a bruise.
This section is for those fighting silent wars,
carrying unseen scars,
and holding onto God with trembling hands.
You are not alone in the valley.

Screaming in the Night

A Poetic Prayer of Lament and Light

I screamed into the hollow dark,
A soul undone, a heart in shards—
"Why have You left me here to break?
Why strike me down with Heaven's guards?"

I tore the silence with my rage,
A storm of blame, a bitter fight—
"My prayers are lost, my hope is gone,
Do You just watch me in the night?"

The stars gave no reply at first,
The moon just stared with ghostly eye—
And still I cried, "Have You no love?
Or is Your mercy just a lie?"

But then… a whisper through the pain,
A breath, a warmth I couldn't see—
The Holy Spirit touched my wounds
And knelt beside the wreck of me.

Not with thunder, not with flame,
Not to rebuke or lecture loud—
But with a light that filled the cracks
And wrapped my soul in healing shroud.

My screams became a river's sob,
The sobs became a salted stream—
And through my tears, a holy hush
Revealed a love that runs unseen.

The warmth grew deep within my chest,
A pulse of peace, a sacred thread—
And faith, once lost, now stirred anew
Where once despair had made its bed.

So now I do not fear the dark,
Nor curse the silence of the skies—
For You are with me in the night,
The God who hears the broken cries.

Scripture Reference
Psalm 34:17–18 (NIV)

"The righteous cry out, and the Lord hears them;
he delivers them from all their troubles.
The Lord is close to the brokenhearted
and saves those who are crushed in spirit."

Where My Demons Hide

A Poetic Prayer for Protection and Grace

Lord, I come not just with praise,
But with the shadows I can't flee—
The parts of me I try to drown,
That still come clawing back to me.

They're quiet when the day is loud,
But whisper sharp when night is near.
They know the cracks, the secret wounds,
They speak in guilt, they thrive in fear.

I smile while they curl inside,
Like serpents coiled in cloaks of shame.
But still they hiss, and still they pull,
And still they call me by my name.

Protect me, Lord, from what I hide—
From bitter thoughts I dare not show.
From urges dark, from poisoned pride,
From seeds I never meant to sow.

I do not ask for You to flee—
But enter in, where most avoid.
Bring light into my hidden rooms,
And fill the hollow with Your voice.

I know they're there. I know You know.
But still I beg You—stay, not run.
Redeem the war within my soul,
And claim the battles I have won.

Let not my demons rule the night.
Let not their whispers guide my hand.
Remind me I am not their own—
I walk within Your promised land.

So when they rise, as demons do,
And press their lies against my mind—
Be louder still, O voice of truth,
My Shepherd fierce, my Savior kind.

Scripture Reference
Psalm 91:9–11 (NIV)

*"If you say, 'The Lord is my refuge,' and you make the Most High your dwelling,
no harm will overtake you, no disaster will come near your tent.
For he will command his angels concerning you to guard you in all your ways."*

Reckoning

A Poetic Prayer from the Edge of Life

I felt the dust return to dust,
My body bowed, my breath unsure—
Each morning felt a final one,
Each night a knock upon death's door.

I made my peace, prepared the scrolls,
Set down my love, unlatched my chest—
I whispered words to those I love,
And tried to leave them with my best.

But still I stayed.
Not strong, not whole—
A flicker faint, a body worn.
And in that place between the veils,
I found a soul reborn.

Was this the wrath I thought You'd send?
Or was it mercy in disguise?
A reckoning, not for my end—
But for the clearing of my eyes?

You didn't come with blinding light,
No angel choir or parting sea—
But in my lowest, weakest hour,
You came, and You remembered me.

You held me close while I broke down,
Rebuilt me slowly, breath by breath—
And though I feared the dark to come,
You wrestled life back out of death.

Now I walk different, think with fire—
Scarred in flesh, but soul refined.
I wear the weight of what I've seen,
Yet leave my bitterness behind.

Perhaps You let me linger here
Because there's more that I must do—
A voice to speak, a hand to lift,
A deeper path to walk with You.

So this, my Lord, is what I bring:
Not answers, pride, or perfect breath—
But gratitude for borrowed days,
For faith found on the edge of death.

Scripture Reference
Psalm 118:17 (NIV)

"I will not die but live, and will proclaim what the Lord has done."

Even Now, I Believe

A Poetic Prayer from the Valley

Even now, when prayers feel lost,
Like ashes scattered on the wind—
When silence echoes louder still
Than every cry I send within—

Even now, I choose to stay.
Though pain has pressed me to the floor,
Though I have questions I can't shape,
And hope feels distant, faint, unsure—

Even now, I speak Your name,
Though not with strength, but weary breath.
Though healing hasn't touched my wound,
Though joy feels buried deep in death.

I do not lift triumphant hands,
Or sing the way I did before—
But I still lift *something*, Lord—
A heart that won't close Heaven's door.

You are not less because I hurt.
You're not untrue because I cry.
You are still God, though I am dust—
Still Savior when I ask You, *why?*

So take my faith, though cracked and thin,
And hold it in Your holy hand.
A mustard seed, a flickered spark—
But still enough to help me stand.

Even now—when all is not
The way I dreamed, the way I pled—
I trust You more than what I feel.
I follow where Your light has led.

And even if I never see
The answer that I ache to find—
Still I believe. Still You are good.
Still I am Yours. Still You are mine.

Scripture Reference
John 11:21–22 (NIV)

"Lord," Martha said to Jesus, "if you had been here, my brother would not have died. But I know that even now God will give you whatever you ask."

The Weary Still Worship

A Poetic Prayer of Sacred Endurance

I don't have songs with perfect pitch,
Or prayers that rise like morning dew.
I've lost the strength to dance or shout—
But still, my heart remembers You.

My hands hang low, my back is bent,
My soul feels bruised from battles long.
But even now, in quiet pain,
I offer You this weary song.

It isn't loud. It isn't bright.
It doesn't flood the air with cheer.
But it is real—it cost me much—
This fragile faith I cradle here.

I worship not with lifted arms,
But with the breath I barely hold.
A whisper in the furnace heat,
A psalm that trembles, faint and bold.

You see the ones who still show up,
Who bless Your name with shaking voice.
Who offer tears instead of gold,
And call that sorrow-laced faith *choice*.

You never asked for flawless songs—
Just hearts that turn to You again.
So take this broken hallelujah,
As one You do not call *less than*.

When strength returns, I'll dance again.
When joy breaks through, I'll raise my hands.
But even if it never comes,
I'll worship still—because I *stand*.

Scripture Reference
Habakkuk 3:17–18 (NIV)

*"Though the fig tree does not bud and there are no grapes on the vines…
yet I will rejoice in the Lord, I will be joyful in God my Savior."*

Stones and Silence

A Poetic Prayer

O Lord who stooped to draw in dust,
While angry voices filled the air—
You saw the shame, you felt the weight,
Yet met it not with wrath, but care.

I hold a stone within my hand,
So quick to cast, so slow to see—
But in Your gaze, the crowd grew still,
And all that judgment turned on me.

Forgive me, Lord, for every time
I've hurled my pride like sharpened stone.
I've stood with Pharisees in thought,
While hiding sins I call my own.

You didn't raise Your voice in rage,
You didn't point or cast me low—
You knelt beside my brokenness,
And whispered grace I didn't know.

"Go now," You said, "and sin no more,"
But not with scorn, not with disdain—
You spoke with love that lifts the soul,
A balm for every hidden pain.

So teach me, Lord, to drop the stones,
To trade my fury for Your peace—
To live as one who's been set free,
And let the voice of mercy speak.

Scripture Reference
John 8:1–11 (NIV)

"Let any one of you who is without sin be the first to throw a stone at her."
... "Woman, where are they? Has no one condemned you?" "No one, sir," she said.
"Then neither do I condemn you," Jesus declared. "Go now and leave your life of sin."

I Am Not My Past

A Poetic Prayer of Identity and Freedom

I've worn the names I never chose—
Mistakes like chains, regret like skin.
I've walked in shadows I called home,
Ashamed of where I've been.

I've let the echoes shape my worth,
Let shame rewrite my sacred name.
But You, O Lord, speak louder still,
And You refuse to play that game.

You don't define me by the scars,
But by the healing that they show.
You see not who I used to be—
But who I'm just beginning to know.

You call me child when I feel fraud,
You call me whole when I feel torn.
You see the day I rise again—
Not just the nights I've sworn and mourned.

So let the past say what it will—
But I am not the lies it speaks.
For grace has written something new
Upon the chapters shame still seeks.

I am not what I have done.
I am not what I have failed.
I am not what darkness claimed—
I am not where fear prevailed.

I am the one You rescued, Lord.
Redeemed by hands that bear the proof.
A temple now, though once in ruins—
A heart rebuilt by sacred truth.

So let this be my battle cry,
When guilt returns like tide and blast—
I am not who I once was.
I am not my past.

Scripture Reference
2 Corinthians 5:17 (NIV)

*"Therefore, if anyone is in Christ, the new creation has come:
The old has gone, the new is here!"*

The Devil Doesn't Get the Last Word

A Poetic Prayer of Holy Defiance

You spoke in lies, in subtle tones,
In whispers laced with guilt and fear.
You tried to bend the truth I knew—
To twist my joy and draw me near.

You came with shame wrapped like a gift,
With doubt disguised in saintly dress.
You told me I was not enough,
Then laughed when I believed it less.

But hear me now, you fallen voice—
You don't define this heart or flame.
Your chains are rust, your power broken.
You'll never steal my Father's name.

I've stumbled, yes—but not undone.
I've wept—but not without my King.
And every scar you tried to carve
Now testifies to better things.

You tried to write my final page—
To end my song with silence deep.
But Heaven held the pen, not you,
And Christ has promises to keep.

The war was waged upon a tree,
And blood was spilled to seal my fate.
But it was not the end, not then—
The stone rolled back. The grave won't wait.

So when you hiss your tired threats,
And haunt me with the sins I've known—
I'll answer not with fear or fight—
But with the cross I call my own.

Because the Author isn't you—
And grace has filled the final line.
The grave is not the final word—
And neither, snake, are you or mine.

Scripture Reference
Romans 16:20 (NIV)

*"The God of peace will soon crush Satan under your feet.
The grace of our Lord Jesus be with you."*

Psalm for the Undone

A Poetic Prayer for the Broken and Beloved

I don't have strength for mighty words,
Or verses carved from perfect breath.
I only have this heart that shakes—
This fragile faith that stares at death.

I am not whole. I'm not composed.
I am not righteous, calm, or wise.
But I still know You hear the cry
That doesn't dress in strong disguise.

So this is all I offer now—
A whispered name, a shaking frame.
No songs, no shouts, no promises—
Just one hand reaching through the flame.

If You are near the crushed and torn,
Then here I am—unfixed, unclean.
Not asking You to make me great,
Just show me that I'm still seen.

They say You love the broken things,
That mercy meets us in the mud.
So let my mess become Your altar,
And meet me here beneath the flood.

Don't fix me fast—just stay awhile.
Don't lecture—just be near and kind.
You are the God of every ache,
Of every heart that's left behind.

And if I never rise like them,
And if my words don't sing like psalms—
Still let me lie here in Your grace,
And feel the safety of Your palms.

Scripture Reference
Psalm 34:18 (NIV)

"The Lord is close to the brokenhearted and saves those who are crushed in spirit."

⚒ The Hands That Build

Work becomes worship. Faith is formed through the tools we hold...

We are makers. Carvers. Carriers.
But our greatest work is often unseen.
These prayers are for those who labor with calloused hands
and holy intentions—who worship in the workshop,
and build what lasts forever.

Between Hammer and Heaven

A Poetic Prayer of Craft and Faith

I build with hands You fashioned first—
With steel and wood, with flame and nail.
I measure twice, I strike with care,
I brace the beam, I drive the rail.

But deeper still, You whisper this:
There's more than what my hands can shape.
A frame of faith, a soul to forge,
A kingdom rising, stair by stair.

For every joint I mortise clean,
You teach me patience, grain by grain.
For every weld I make to hold,
You bind my heart through joy and pain.

You were a carpenter, O Christ—
A craftsman born of humble grace.
And yet You built beyond the wood,
A love the world could not erase.

So let my labor be a prayer,
Each cut and carve a sacred rite—
That what I build in flesh and form
Reflects the work I build in light.

With every board, a deeper trust.
With every nail, a prayer secured.
With every plan, a leap of faith.
With every flaw, Your grace endured.

Shape me, Lord, as I shape the frame—
Not just a house, but holy place.
Let every tool remind my soul
That I am built by hands of grace.

Scripture Reference
1 Corinthians 3:10–11 (NIV)

"By the grace God has given me, I laid a foundation as a wise builder...
For no one can lay any foundation other than the one already laid, which is Jesus Christ."

With These Hands

A Poetic Prayer of Work and Worship

With these hands, I've shaped and carved,
Built frames of wood and welded steel.
I've wiped away the sweat and tears,
And prayed through pain I couldn't feel.

These hands have held, and sometimes hurt,
Have built up walls, and torn them down.
They've reached in love and clenched in rage—
They've known both blessing and the frown.

But now I raise them, rough and worn,
Not in defense, but in surrender—
To offer all I've made and marred
To You, the Giver and Defender.

Use these hands to heal, not harm—
To lift the weak, to serve the small.
To steady hearts when storms arise,
To brace the weight when others fall.

Let these hands plant seeds of peace,
Shape truth in words, and grace in deed.
To touch the lives I may not know,
But whom You place within my reach.

I may not preach from mountaintops,
Or write the songs the angels sing—
But if these hands can build Your house,
Then let them craft eternal things.

And when they still, at journey's end,
Let it be known, without applause—
These hands were Yours from start to close,
And labored always for Your cause.

Scripture Reference
Colossians 3:23–24 (NIV)

"Whatever you do, work at it with all your heart, as working for the Lord, not for human masters…
It is the Lord Christ you are serving."

The Sacred Ordinary

A Poetic Prayer for Everyday Holiness

I wake before the world is loud,
Before the traffic shakes the ground.
I brew my coffee, lace my boots,
And feel Your presence all around.

There's nothing grand about this day—
No mountaintop, no parted sea.
Just lists to check, and tools to lift,
But still… I know You walk with me.

You bless the moments no one sees—
The sweeping floor, the folded sheet.
The way I listen, love, and try,
The kindness tucked in small defeats.

This isn't fire from the sky—
It's grace in every breath I take.
The sacred lives between the lines
Of every move I choose to make.

You're in the sink, the hammer's swing,
The phone call made, the quiet chore.
You turn the mundane into gold—
You make the "less" become the *more*.

So let me not despise this pace,
These daily tasks, these silent hours.
For You are here within them all,
And You alone give them their power.

And when I lay my head to rest,
Let it be said, "I walked with God."
Not in the fire or the storm—
But in the sacred, common sod.

Scripture Reference
Zechariah 4:10 (NLT)

"Do not despise these small beginnings, for the Lord rejoices to see the work begin..."

Work Is Worship

A Poetic Prayer of Devoted Doing

Not every prayer is wrapped in words,
Not every hymn is sung out loud.
Sometimes it's in the weight I lift,
The sweat I wear instead of shroud.

The time clock doesn't seem like church,
The noise of life, no sacred sound—
But still I feel You standing near,
Each time my feet are on the ground.

The work I do—though rough, unseen—
Becomes a song when done for You.
Each task, a note of love declared,
Each chore, a spark of something true.

You shaped the world with hands and breath,
With form and function, sweat and light.
So let me meet You in my day,
And serve with heart and hammer tight.

If I must labor, let it bless.
If I must build, let it restore.
If I must serve, let it reflect
The One who washed the feet before.

Let dishes scrubbed and boards aligned,
Be holy as a prophet's prayer.
Let factory floor and apron tied
Be altars where I'm made aware—

That every task I do with love,
With honesty, with grace and care,
Becomes a gift, a sacred act—
A quiet way to lift You there.

Scripture Reference
Colossians 3:17 (NIV)

"And whatever you do, whether in word or deed, do it all in the name of the Lord Jesus…"

Teach Me to Build Like You

A Poetic Prayer to the Carpenter King

You built with calloused, steady hands,
With wood and sweat, with dust and flame.
You shaped the world in quiet ways,
Before the world had learned Your name.

And still You build—not just with nails,
But with compassion, truth, and light.
You framed a Kingdom with Your love,
And held it firm through darkest night.

So teach me, Lord, to build like You—
Not just with strength, but grace and care.
To see the soul behind the task,
To leave Your fingerprints out there.

Teach me to measure more than beams,
To level hearts, not just the line.
To chisel out what pride has carved,
And sand my anger down to kind.

Let every plan be drawn in prayer.
Let every nail be placed with peace.
Let every corner I construct
Make room for hope that won't decrease.

And when my hands begin to fail,
When sweat outpaces sacred pace—
Remind me I am not alone—
Your Spirit works in every space.

O Master Craftsman of my soul,
You shaped the stars, yet worked with wood.
So build in me a life that stands—
And let it all be called *very good*.

Scripture Reference
Ephesians 2:10 (NIV)

"For we are God's handiwork, created in Christ Jesus to do good works, which God prepared in advance for us to do."

Blueprints and Bruises

A Poetic Prayer for When the Plan Falls Apart

I drew the lines with careful hand,
I measured twice, I thought it through.
I laid the plans, I built the frame—
And watched it all collapse anew.

The dreams I shaped with blood and breath
Now lie in splinters at my feet.
And all my "sure" turned into "why,"
As heaven's silence filled the street.

But still I hear You in the dust,
Not with a scold, but with a sigh—
You kneel beside the mess I made,
And whisper, *"Let's give it one more try."*

You are the Architect of grace,
Who drafts with love and builds with light.
You see the beauty through the breaks,
The strength beneath the sleepless night.

So teach me not to curse the fall,
Or hate the flaws that slow me down.
For even bruises bear Your print,
And plans may change, but not Your crown.

Let every broken beam remind
That I am not the one who saves.
But I can build what You design,
And trust You, even through the graves.

Scripture Reference
Proverbs 16:9 (NIV)

"In their hearts humans plan their course, but the Lord establishes their steps."

Sanctified Sweat

A Poetic Prayer of Grit and Grace

This isn't hallelujah loud,
No stained glass or cathedral dome—
Just boots that echo down the hall,
A tired man making grace his home.

No spotlight shines on folding chairs,
Or busted knuckles, aching bones.
But still You meet me in this place—
Where worship wears its work clothes.

The hammer swing, the silent tears,
The long shift with no thanks in sight—
These aren't small things, not to You—
They're sacred, in Your perfect light.

You made the sweat upon my brow,
You called the weary ones Your own.
You washed the feet of those who serve—
And built a Kingdom stone by stone.

So when I lift what no one sees,
When I keep going, beat and bruised—
Remind me that You see it all,
And not a moment goes unused.

Let every ache become a song,
Each breath a line in Heaven's psalm.
Let even silence praise Your name—
For You are here, and I am calm.

This life is holy, hour by hour,
Not just in pews, but in the dust.
And if this sweat is sanctified,
Then let me serve and never rust.

Scripture Reference
Galatians 6:9 (NIV)

"Let us not become weary in doing good, for at the proper time we will reap a harvest if we do not give up."

Nails and Names

A Poetic Prayer of Sacrifice and Identity

With these hands, I've driven nails,
To hold up frames, to build, to bind—
But in the quiet, I recall
Another set—of different kind.

You too have known the iron bite,
The echo of a splintered beam.
But Yours were not for walls or roofs—
They held the weight of all my dreams.

They held the weight of every lie,
Each burden I could never lift.
And through those wounds, You wrote my name—
A sacred, blood-bound, holy gift.

So now I build, but not for pride—
Not just for pay or passing fame.
Each nail I drive reminds my heart:
I bear Your scars, I wear Your name.

Let what I make reflect Your love—
Let how I work reveal Your grace.
And when I doubt my worth or role,
Remind me of that rugged place.

Where hands were pierced to make me whole,
And wood was raised to set me free—
Where sacrifice became a name,
And now that name belongs to me.

So use these hands, though rough and flawed,
To honor what Your cross has done.
For every nail I press with care,
I'm praising Christ, the Risen Son.

Scripture Reference
Isaiah 49:16 (NIV)

"See, I have engraved you on the palms of my hands; your walls are ever before me."

👑 The Kingdom Above and Within

Heaven is not only what we wait for—it's what we're becoming...

The Kingdom of God is not a far-off castle.
It's here. It's now. It's within you.
These poems lift the eyes, stir the heart,
and remind the soul that eternity is breaking through
the cracks of today.

The Kingdom Above

A Poetic Prayer of Longing and Hope

O Lord of stars and sovereign skies,
Whose throne no time or thief can move—
I lift my eyes beyond the clouds
To glimpse the Kingdom from above.

Not brick or blade, nor throne of man,
Not gold that fades or crowns that rust—
But joy untouched by sorrow's hand,
And peace that does not break or bust.

We speak of streets that shine like glass,
Of gates like pearl, of endless light—
But more than walls or jeweled halls,
I long to dwell within Your sight.

Is there a place beyond this pain?
A realm where every tear is dry?
Where all our sighs become a song,
And faith no longer wonders why?

You said it once, and still it stands—
The Kingdom's near, yet still to come.
It lives within the hearts of those
Who walk with Christ, the risen Son.

So let my heart not chase the dust,
Or build on sand that slides away.
Let me, instead, invest in hope—
And plant my soul where You will stay.

Until that day when skies are torn,
And Heaven's gates swing wide with grace—
Prepare my hands, prepare my heart
To serve until I see Your face.

Scripture Reference
Hebrews 12:28 (NIV)

"Therefore, since we are receiving a kingdom that cannot be shaken, let us be thankful, and so worship God acceptably with reverence and awe."

Built for Eternity

A Poetic Prayer of Lasting Purpose

The world says build what fades with time—
Stack bricks of wealth and climb your name.
But every tower here will fall,
And every spotlight dims the flame.

So let me build what time can't touch,
Not monuments of stone or gold—
But acts of love, and seeds of truth,
That rise when earthly stories fold.

Let my foundation be Your word,
My blueprint drawn in holy light.
For though the storms may bend the beams,
What's built in You will still stand right.

Not for applause or fleeting fame,
But for the glory only Yours—
A shelter in another's storm,
A welcome at the stranger's doors.

Each prayer I pray, each hand I lend,
Each tear I trust You'll one day dry—
Be part of something more than me—
A kingdom I can't quantify.

So help me build with Heaven's tools,
To trade short gain for lasting worth—
And labor not for dust and rust,
But what outlives this mortal earth.

When breath is gone and nails fall still,
And I have done all I can do—
Let me be known not by what *lasts*,
But by what *leads the soul to You*.

Scripture Reference
Matthew 6:19–20 (NIV)

"Do not store up for yourselves treasures on earth... but store up for yourselves treasures in heaven...
For where your treasure is, there your heart will be also."

When I Meet God

A Poetic Prayer of the First Face-to-Face

How will I stand, or will I fall,
When all of Heaven hears my name?
Will silence wrap around my soul,
Or will I shout and feel no shame?

Will I be child, or kneeling saint?
Will tears like rivers trace my face?
Will laughter burst like morning light
Within the presence of Your grace?

Will words betray me, lost and weak,
When I behold eternal flame?
Will I recall my earthly doubts,
Or will Your glory cleanse my shame?

Will angels pause their ceaseless song
To watch a wanderer come home?
Will I remember every scar—
Or will You say, "You're not alone"?

Will I be welcomed as I am,
Though frail of faith and rough of soul?
Will I still fear, or feel fulfilled?
Will being there at last make whole?

You know, O Lord, the time, the place—
The hour You'll draw the veil aside.
But let my heart rehearse with hope
The day my soul is glorified.

And if I cry, let it be joy.
And if I kneel, let it be grace.
And if I run, then let it be
Into the arms I long to face.

Scripture Reference
1 John 3:2 (NIV)

"Dear friends, now we are children of God, and what we will be has not yet been made known.
But we know that when Christ appears, we shall be like him, for we shall see him as he is."

When You Meet Me

A Poetic Reflection from the Father's Heart

I saw you long before your birth,
Before the world had learned your name.
I shaped your soul with tender care—
No flaw, no fault, no trace of shame.

I watched you stumble, watched you rise,
Heard every prayer you thought too small.
I counted every tear you wept,
And caught them—each and all.

You feared My wrath, but knew not yet
That all I longed for was your face.
Not perfect words, but honest heart—
Not pride, but need, not law, but grace.

And when your feet begin to near
The gates My mercy forged in flame—
I'll run to you. Yes, *run*—not wait—
And call you home, and speak your name.

I will not ask you for a speech,
Or hold your sins for all to see.
My Son has borne them, every one—
Your debt is gone. You're home with Me.

I will not thunder blame or fear.
I'll lift your chin, I'll meet your eye.
And you will know—without one word—
How long I've loved, how hard I've tried.

Perhaps you'll cry. Perhaps you'll fall.
Perhaps you'll simply breathe at last.
But I will hold you, child of dust—
And all your pain will come to pass.

And if you run, then I will too.
And if you sing, I'll sing along.
And if you kneel, I'll lift you up—
For you are Mine. You *always* belonged.

Scripture Reference
Luke 15:20 (NIV)

"But while he was still a long way off, his father saw him and was filled with compassion for him;
he ran to his son, threw his arms around him and kissed him."

One Day Soon

A Poetic Prayer of Eternal Hope

One day soon, the sky will break—
Not with storm, but sacred light.
And all the shadows we have feared
Will vanish in the blaze of right.

One day soon, the trumpet sounds,
And graves will give up all they hold.
The tear-stained earth will lift her eyes
To joy no sorrow can withhold.

One day soon, the veil will tear,
Not temple cloth, but time itself—
And we will see what faith foresaw,
What prophets spoke, not for themselves.

One day soon, the pain will pass,
The war inside will cease to roar.
No more goodbyes, no final breath—
Just home, and love forevermore.

I do not know the hour or day,
Or how the heavens will unfold—
But still I feel the rising hush
Of promises more strong than gold.

So help me live like this is true—
To love, forgive, endure, and pray.
To walk with grace, to hold with hope,
And bless the world along the way.

And when You come, or call me home,
Let it not catch me unaware—
But as a child who knows the sound
Of Father's footsteps on the stair.

Scripture Reference
Revelation 21:4–5 (NIV)

"He will wipe every tear from their eyes. There will be no more death or mourning or crying or pain,
for the old order of things has passed away."
He who was seated on the throne said, "I am making everything new!"

Until the Trumpet Sounds

A Poetic Prayer of Holy Readiness

I walk this world with eyes upturned,
A pilgrim on a road of dust.
I build, I bless, I break, I mend—
But never place my full-born trust.

For something stirs beneath the wind,
A sound not heard, but deeply known—
A whisper carried through the years,
A call to bring the wanderers home.

I do not know the hour, Lord,
Nor how the heavens will be split—
But still I live like it is near,
And let my soul stay candle-lit.

I'll love with urgency and grace,
I'll serve as if the time is short—
For every kindness is a seed
That testifies in Heaven's court.

I'll keep my hands upon the plow,
My heart awake, my spirit sound—
And run this race until the day
I hear that final trumpet sound.

And when it comes, I won't look back—
No fear, no shame, no earthly claim.
For all I've done, I've done for You—
And You alone will speak my name.

So keep me faithful, keep me clean,
Keep oil burning in my flame—
Until I rise to meet the One
Who knows and calls me just the same.

Scripture Reference
1 Thessalonians 4:16–17 (NIV)

*"For the Lord himself will come down from heaven, with a loud command,
with the voice of the archangel and with the trumpet call of God…
And so we will be with the Lord forever."*

The Kingdom in Me

A Poetic Prayer of Present Glory

I looked for Heaven in the sky,
In streets of gold, in gates of flame—
In thrones and choirs, and angels' wings,
In visions shaped by sacred name.

But then You whispered in my soul,
Not from above, but deep within:
"The Kingdom isn't far away—
It starts right now, beneath your skin."

It lives in how I speak and love,
In how I serve and choose to stay.
It's found in tears I wipe away,
And peace I carry through the day.

It's in the mercy I extend,
In truth I hold when lies surround.
It's in the justice I pursue
When silence echoes all around.

It's in the prayer I barely speak,
The faith I live but rarely show—
The choice to bless instead of curse,
To build when I could just let go.

You are the King—my heart, Your throne.
Your Spirit, planted seed by seed,
Now grows within this common ground
To meet the world's uncommon need.

So let me walk as one who knows
That Heaven isn't far or free—
But breaking through, with every step,
Wherever You have placed the Kingdom in me.

Scripture Reference
Luke 17:21 (NIV)

"…the kingdom of God is in your midst."

❧ Let It Be So

A final blessing. A holy yes.

After the questions, the cries, the work, and the worship—
we come to rest.
These final words are not an ending,
but an agreement with Heaven.
A sacred exhale. A whispered amen.
Let it be so.

Let It Be So

A Poetic Benediction

To every prayer I've cried in dark,
To every joy I've dared to know—
To all You've done and still will do—
O Lord my God, let it be so.

To faith that flickers, yet still fights,
To mercy I could never earn,
To grace that found me in the dust,
And taught my soul again to burn—

To every word You've breathed through pain,
To every silence shaped by light—
To all the ways You stayed with me
When nothing else was going right—

To love that breaks and makes me new,
To peace that walks where I have bled,
To hope that waits beyond the grave,
To life that rises from the dead—

To all You are and all I'll be,
To every seed I've yet to sow—
To every yes I've whispered weak—
O faithful God, let it be so.

Scripture Reference
2 Corinthians 1:20 (NIV)

"For no matter how many promises God has made, they are 'Yes' in Christ. And so through him the 'Amen' is spoken by us to the glory of God."

Part II

Songs for the Last Sunrise

Poetic Prayers for the End of Night and the Coming of Light

"The night is nearly over;
the day is almost here…"
— Romans 13:12 (NIV)

Foreword

Songs for the Last Sunrise was never meant to be pretty.
It was meant to be **true**.

These are not polished prayers.
They are the groanings of a heart that's waited, watched, broken, and still believed.

This book is for the weary ones who never stopped hoping.
For the ones who walked through fire and still carry the smell of smoke on their soul.
For those who have stood watch while the world slept,
who've stared into the silence and whispered,
"Even now... I believe."

These are songs for the final hours.
For the morning when the King returns.
For the last sunrise—
when faith becomes sight,
and we rise with Him.

📖 Part 2: Table of Content

Section I: Nightfall

Where faith flickers and the shadows speak.

The sun has slipped beneath the line.
The world is quiet, but not at peace.
This is where hope grows tired,
and faith learns to breathe in the dark.
These are prayers for the soul that hasn't let go—
but doesn't know how much longer it can hold on.

Live Like You Were Dying

A Poetic Prayer of Urgent Grace

If today was borrowed breath,
And tomorrow never came—
Would you still wait to say *I'm sorry*,
Still play silence like a game?

Would you still chase things that rust,
Still bite your tongue when love should speak?
Would you still scroll instead of hold,
Still hoard your words from those who're weak?

If the clock began to shout,
And death stood close—not just in threat—
Would you rise and run toward living?
Would you dance with no regret?

Would you give more grace than grudge?
Would you laugh until it aches?
Would you kiss the ones you're near
And let your soul make no mistakes?

Because I have tasted almost gone.
I've felt the night press on my chest.
And now I know what most forget—
That **living fully is a test**.

So I will love like time is short.
I will build like Heaven sees.
I will speak like it's my last chance
To set another captive free.

I will pray without pretending.
I will walk without disguise.
I will cry if I am broken—
And still dare to hope *and rise*.

For I have seen the fragile edge
Where all I planned fades into mist.
And now I choose—before it's gone—
To live the life I almost missed.

So Lord, remind me every breath
Could be the last one in this skin.
And let me live not scared of dying—
But bold enough to *truly begin*.

Scripture Reference
Psalm 90:12 (NIV)

*"Teach us to number our days,
that we may gain a heart of wisdom."*

The Silence Before the Trumpet

A Poetic Prayer of Holy Anticipation

There's a stillness in the sky tonight—
not empty,
but expectant.
Like creation is holding its breath,
waiting for something we can't yet name.

The wind has quieted.
The noise of man,
dimmed to a hum.
And somewhere deep within my bones,
I feel it coming.

The sound.

The shift.

The trumpet.

But it has not blown—
not yet.
And so we wait,
lamps trimmed,
hearts pressed to the threshold of forever.

This is not fear.
It's not panic.
It's that sacred hush before the wedding begins,
before the battle trumpet sounds,
before the King steps through the veil.

And so I listen.
And I watch.

And I pray—
not for more time,
but for the wisdom to spend what's left

in love,
in light,
in truth.

Lord, if this is the silence before the trumpet,
then let me not waste it in slumber.
Let me live like a flame still lit.
Let me forgive what should be forgiven.
Let me speak what still needs said.
Let me stand at the edge of eternity
with my soul wide open.

Because when the sound comes—
when the sky splits,
and the trumpet sings—
I want to rise,
not run.

I want to rejoice,
not regret.

So teach me how to honor this silence,
and make me ready
for the sound.

Scripture Reference
1 Thessalonians 5:6 (NIV)

"So then, let us not be like others, who are asleep, but let us be awake and sober."

When Hope Went Quiet

A Poetic Prayer in the Pause

There was a time I sang to You,
With fire in my breath,
With praise that burned like morning light,
And joy that danced with death.

But something shifted in the dark—
A silence came,
Not full of fear,
But heavy,
Like the hush before a storm,
Or the pause before a tear.

I didn't lose my faith, not quite.
I didn't curse or run.
But somewhere deep within my chest,
The shouting came undone.

My hope went quiet.

Not gone,
But still.
Not lost,
But low.
Like a flame in its final flicker—
Still there, but aching slow.

I wanted thunder.
I wanted signs.
Instead, You offered breath.
Just breath.
And asked me to believe
without the blaze I used to know.

So here I am, Lord—
Not loud,

Not proud,
But real.

Still holding something sacred
Even when it won't ignite.
Still here in the silence
Where faith forgets its fight.

I know You're not offended
By the stillness in my soul.
I know You've waited in this quiet
Long before the stories told.

So stay with me in this moment.
In the pause that speaks in sighs.
And teach me how to worship
Even when the hallelujah hides.

Scripture Reference
Romans 8:26 (NIV)
"The Spirit helps us in our weakness. We do not know what we ought to pray for, but the Spirit himself intercedes for us through wordless groans."

The End of My Strength

A Poetic Prayer of Surrender and Survival

I've carried more than I should have,
Lifted burdens I called mine.
I've worn a face of quiet fight,
And told the world, *"I'm fine."*

But here—
Here at the end of what I have,
Where sleep forgets to come,
And thoughts run wild in midnight loops
Of everything undone—

I can't pretend I'm strong right now.
I won't.

I'm tired.
Tired in my bones.
Tired in my prayers.
Tired of being the one who stands
When no one else is there.

And yet—
You do not fault me
For the faltering of my frame.
You do not shame me
For the weight I cannot name.

Instead, You kneel beside me.
Not to scold, but to sustain.
You gather up my final breath
And breathe it back again.

You never asked for perfect strength—
Just presence.
Just the will to say,
*"Lord, if You still have room for me,
then carry me today."*

So I will lay down every fight
I'm too weak now to win.
And trust You not to walk away,
But meet me where I end.

Because where my power disappears—
Yours begins to shine.
And at the end of all I have,
I'm found in what is Thine.

Scripture Reference
2 Corinthians 12:9 (NIV)

"My grace is sufficient for you, for my power is made perfect in weakness."

Echoes in the Ashes

A Poetic Lament for What Was Lost

The fire is out.
Not with violence,
but with time.
It burned bright once—
so bright it blinded,
so fierce it warmed everyone near.

But now,
only ashes.

Cold.
Still.
Sacred.

I run my hand through what remains—
the dust of dreams,
the soot of prayers once shouted,
the bones of plans
that never reached their finish.

And yet—
I swear I still hear something.
Not voices,
but echoes.
Like the walls still remember
what it felt like to be home.

Like the laughter
once baked into the boards
hasn't fully faded yet.

I hear the names of people I've lost
in the cracks of the silence.
I feel their fingerprints
on the fragile pages of my memory.

Gone… but still here
in the echoes.

The ashes do not lie—
but they do not get the final word.

There's beauty even in the breakage,
truth even in the ruin.
Not everything that's fallen
was wasted.

So I bless the flame for what it gave,
I weep for what it took,
And I leave this place
with ash on my skin
and grace in my steps.

Still marked.
Still moved.
Still listening
to the echoes in the ashes.

Scripture Reference
Isaiah 61:3 (NIV)

"…to bestow on them a crown of beauty instead of ashes,
the oil of joy instead of mourning,
and a garment of praise instead of a spirit of despair."

Worn Thin but Still Here

A Poetic Prayer of Grit and Grace

I don't have fresh strength today.
I'm not bursting with belief,
or dancing through my trials
like some polished version of praise.

I'm just… here.

Worn thin.
Edges frayed.
Hope like fabric pulled too tight
over weeks that never quite healed right.

But still—
I breathe.
I rise.
I stay.

That has to count for something, doesn't it?

Because faith isn't always fire.
Sometimes it's just a flicker
that won't go out.
Sometimes it's a hand held steady
even when the heart wants to fold.

I'm not strong today, Lord.
But I showed up.
And I'm still reaching for You
even when my grip shakes.

You never asked me for perfection.
You asked me to remain.
So here I am—
worn thin…
but still Yours.

Still here.
Still reaching.
Still believing that You see me
in the stretch of this silence,
in the press of this pain.

So let my staying be worship.
Let my breath be enough.
Let my scraped knees be altars,
and my tired soul be
holy ground.

Scripture Reference
Galatians 6:9 (NIV)

*"Let us not become weary in doing good,
for at the proper time we will reap a harvest if we do not give up."*

The Moon Still Rises

A Poetic Benediction for the Long Night

The sun has slipped beyond the hills,
and shadows now have come to stay.
The sky wears mourning like a veil,
and still…
I wait.
I pray.

The day is done.
The light is gone.
The warmth I knew has grown unsure.
But even in this cold descent,
I sense a hush that feels like *more*.

Because though the sun has fled the sky,
its echoes linger in the air—
reflected softly in the dark
by one who rises,
always there.

The moon still rises.
Quiet. Slow.
A borrowed flame,
a subtle grace.
Not blazing, no—
but still enough
to light this path,
to mark this place.

So if you find yourself in night,
in ache, in silence, in retreat—
remember this:
the dark is not
the only thing beneath your feet.

For even here,
where hope feels thin,
and every prayer is wrapped in why—
the moon still rises,
God still speaks,
and stars are waiting
in the sky.

Scripture Reference
Psalm 139:11–12 (NIV)

*"If I say, 'Surely the darkness will hide me
and the light become night around me,'
even the darkness will not be dark to you…"*

🔥 Section II: Smoke and Ember

What's left after the fire. What still burns.

The fire has passed.
Not everything survived.
But something still glows—
in the ashes, in the scars,
in the hands that still rise.
These are prayers from the aftermath—
not polished, but purified.

"Forgive Me for the Delays"

A Poetic Prayer of Hesitation and Grace

Lord,
I know You called me long ago.
Before the smoke,
before the slip,
before the thousand tiny "not yets"
that turned into
years.

You whispered.
You opened doors.
You sent signs I chose not to follow.
And still,
You stayed.

So now, here in the quiet
after the wreck,
when the echo of Your mercy is louder
than my excuses,
I kneel.

Not proud.
Not polished.
Just present.

Forgive me for the delays, Lord.
For thinking I had more time.
For silencing the stirrings
and burying the call beneath comfort.

Forgive me for waiting until the fire came
to finally listen.

And thank You—
for not walking away
when I made You wait.

You never stopped preparing the road
even when I paused at every turn.
You never stopped believing
in what You planted.

So now,
with what's left of my hands,
and what's whole in my heart,
I say yes.

Even late.
Even tired.
Even scarred.

Yes.

Scripture Reference
2 Peter 3:9 (NIV)

"The Lord is not slow in keeping his promise... He is patient with you."

The Things I Let Burn

A Poetic Prayer of Surrender

Lord,
I didn't lose these things.
I let them burn.

I laid them down in flames—
the pride I wore like armor,
the bitterness I fed like bread,
the image I tried so hard to protect
when I was breaking underneath it.

They didn't go quietly.
I had to watch them twist in the fire—
dreams I swore were from You,
control I thought was wisdom,
plans that had my name
but not Your breath.

I wanted to save them.
I did.
But You were not in the saving—
You were in the letting go.

So I opened my hands,
even as they shook.
I turned from the smoke,
even as it stung.

And I watched
what was never meant to carry me
turn to ash
at Your feet.

Not everything that burned was evil.
Some of it was just... extra.
Unnecessary.

Good things that couldn't go
where You're calling me now.

So I thank You for the fire,
even as it stripped me.
I bless the flame
that made me lighter,
truer,
free.

And now, I walk forward
with the scent of smoke in my hair,
but no chains on my soul.

I am not what I lost.
I am what I laid down.

And what remains
is ready to rise.

Scripture Reference
Hebrews 12:27–28 (NIV)

"...so that what cannot be shaken may remain.
Therefore, since we are receiving a kingdom that cannot be shaken, let us be thankful..."

When I Finally Fell Apart

A Poetic Prayer of Broken Surrender

Lord,
I tried to hold it all together.
Tried to tape the cracks,
to patch the seams,
to keep the mask from slipping
while everything underneath me gave way.

I called it strength.
You called it fear.

I called it discipline.
You saw the desperate strain.

But the day came—
quiet,
heavy,
holy—
when the scaffolding collapsed
and I finally fell
apart.

And You didn't flinch.
You didn't scold.
You didn't say, *"I told you so."*

You just sat with me
in the ruins.

You let me weep.
You let me ache.
You let me grieve what I'd been carrying
longer than I was ever meant to.

You held me,
not in judgment,
but in gentleness.

And as the pieces rested at Your feet,
I began to believe—
not in my ability to rebuild,
but in **Your willingness to remain**.

So I thank You
not just for healing me,
but for letting me be broken
without shame.

Because in the falling,
You met me fully.

And in the breaking,
You began the blessing.

Scripture Reference
Psalm 34:18 (NIV)

*"The Lord is close to the brokenhearted
and saves those who are crushed in spirit."*

Ashes on My Hands

A Poetic Prayer of Surviving the Fire

Lord,
I didn't come through the fire unscathed.
I didn't walk out shiny,
or whole,
or singing a victory song.

I walked out with **ashes on my hands**.

Remnants.
Marks.
Proof.

Of what I carried,
Of what I lost,
Of what I never want to carry again.

There are parts of me
I had to leave in the flames—
anger,
ego,
the illusion that I was fine.

And though I made it through,
I made it through *scarred.*
Smudged.
Changed.

Some people hide their burns.
Try to wash off the smoke.
Pretend the heat didn't touch them.

But I wear my ashes
like a testimony.

Not because I'm proud
of what I walked through,

but because I'm **grateful**
for who I became in the fire.

You didn't leave me there.
You didn't let it consume me.
You walked me out—
slowly,
patiently,
faithfully.

And now,
when I lift my hands to pray,
I see the traces still.

And I remember—
You were with me
even then.

So I'll bless these ashes, Lord.
They remind me
that the fire came,
but it didn't win.

And neither did I—
You did.

Scripture Reference
Isaiah 43:2 (NIV)

*"When you walk through the fire, you will not be burned;
the flames will not set you ablaze."*

I Miss Who I Was Before the Fire

A Poetic Prayer of Honest Grief

Lord,
I don't regret the growth—
but I miss the man
who hadn't yet been broken.

I miss the ease,
the innocence,
the belief that faith would shield me
from the flame.

Before the fire,
I thought strength meant never bending.
That tears were failure,
and surrender was weakness
dressed in soft excuses.

I miss the confidence—
even if it was built on sand.
The clarity—
even if it came from not yet knowing
what the storm would cost.

But now…
I know too much
to pretend.

The fire took
some of what I loved,
some of who I was,
and things I can never quite get back.

And yet—
You do not fault me for the ache.
You do not shame the shadow
I still carry from those flames.

You sit with me in the aftermath,
and whisper,
"I know."

I miss who I was before the fire…
but I'm learning to bless
who I've become because of it.

A little softer.
A little slower.
A little more like someone
who's held by grace
instead of propped up by pride.

So if the fire
was the only way
to find this version of me—
then I'll mourn the old
and walk with the new.

Still scarred.
Still sacred.
Still Yours.

Scripture Reference
1 Peter 1:6–7 (NIV)

"…though now for a little while you may have had to suffer grief…
These have come so that the proven genuineness of your faith—of greater worth than gold,
which perishes even though refined by fire—may result in praise, glory and honor…"

The Fire Was the Answer

A Poetic Prayer of Holy Clarity

I asked You for rescue.
You gave me fire.

I prayed for peace.
You handed me a storm.

I begged for escape.
You said,
"No—this is the way through."

And I didn't understand.

I thought You had turned away,
left me in the blaze
with nothing but unanswered prayers
and scorched faith.

But now—
with ash behind me
and new breath in my lungs—
I see it.

The fire was the answer.

Not the punishment.
Not the silence.
Not the failure of Your love—
but the *proving of it.*

It burned away what couldn't last.
It refined what was buried.
It tested the frame of who I thought I was
and showed me what could truly hold.

I see now—
how gold is never born,

only revealed
by heat.

And I am not who I was before the flame.

So thank You—
for what You didn't spare me from,
but stood with me inside of.

Thank You—
for the tears,
the blaze,
the brokenness…

and the beauty
that came after.

You didn't leave me in the fire.
You left part of me *there*.
And what walked out
was something stronger,
brighter,
and finally real.

Scripture Reference
Isaiah 48:10 (NIV)

"See, I have refined you… I have tested you in the furnace of affliction."

Still Glowing

A Poetic Prayer of Gentle Endurance

Lord,
I'm not blazing anymore.
Not like I used to.

The fire that once lit every step
has quieted to something smaller—
softer.
A glow.

And maybe that's the point.

Because the blaze was beautiful,
but the embers are faithful.
They last.
They stay.

I've walked through the heat.
I've wept in the smoke.
I've buried things I thought I needed
just to make it out alive.

And still…
here I am.
Not loud.
Not triumphant.
But **still glowing**.

Still carrying light
from the God who didn't ask me
to be brilliant every day—
just to keep burning.

Even now,
in the aftermath,
You sit with me by the coals.
You warm my soul

with quiet grace.
You call this glow *worship*.

So let this be my praise:
Not fireworks.
Not thunder.
Just this slow, steady flame
that says,
"I'm still Yours."

Scripture Reference
Matthew 12:20 (NIV)

"A bruised reed he will not break,
and a smoldering wick he will not snuff out…"

🛡 Section III: Watchmen on the Wall

The voices that wait, warn, and won't be moved.

Some leave the wall.
Some fall asleep.
But a few remain—
oil in their lamps,
eyes on the horizon,
hearts that still cry out,
"He is coming."
These are prayers from the watchtower—
urgent, unwavering, awake.

Keep Your Oil Lit

A Poetic Prayer of Readiness

Lord,
I feel the world slowing down,
settling into slumber.
Voices growing dull,
hearts growing cold.
And still, You whisper—
"Stay ready."

So I keep watch.
Not with fear,
but with fire.

I trim the wick,
pour the oil,
and set my soul to burn
a little longer.

Because I don't know the hour.
You never gave me that.
But You gave me a lamp—
and told me to keep it lit.

So here I am,
in the middle of the night,
faith flickering,
but not failing.

I won't let the silence
steal my spark.
I won't let the delay
extinguish my devotion.

Let me be the one
who waits well.
Who loves without sleeping.
Who watches without wavering.

Even if the others fade,
even if the crowd forgets,
even if I burn alone—
I will burn
for You.

Because when You come,
I want to be found
ready.

Still glowing.
Still awake.
Still filled
with oil and hope.

Scripture Reference
Matthew 25:13 (NIV)

"Therefore keep watch, because you do not know the day or the hour."

If This Was the Last Psalm

A Poetic Prayer of Final Praise

Lord,
If this was the last psalm I ever prayed—
no encore,
no reply,
no second chance to rewrite the lines—

let it say what matters.

Let it speak of **mercy**,
not my merit.

Let it echo **grace**,
not my guilt.

Let it sing, even if my voice shakes,
that **You were faithful**
when I was frail,
and good
when I could not see the good at all.

If this was the last psalm,
I wouldn't ask for answers—
just a hand to hold.
I wouldn't rage at the dark—
I'd light one more flame
and set it on the windowsill for someone else.

If this was the last psalm,
let it be a whisper
that cuts through the noise.
A breath that carries
more surrender than sound.

Let it be love.
Let it be peace.
Let it be the sound of a soul

that still believes
even after everything.

And if this is the last time You hear me say it,
then hear me clearly:

I am Yours.
I was always Yours.
And I will still be singing
when breath is done.

Scripture Reference
Psalm 104:33 (NIV)

"I will sing to the Lord all my life;
I will sing praise to my God as long as I live."

I Will Not Look Away

A Poetic Prayer of Courageous Compassion

Lord,
I see what others choose to miss.

The pain
The hunger
The hands reaching out
while the world pulls its shades.

I see the cracks
in perfect smiles.
The ache beneath
the laughter shared online.

I see the blood
on broken streets.
The weeping
no one livestreams.

And I won't
look away.

Not because I'm stronger.
Not because I know what to do.
But because **You didn't**
when You saw *me*.

When I was the wounded,
the weary,
the forgotten—
You looked.
You stopped.
You stayed.

So teach me to carry the ache
without being crushed by it.

To hold the sorrow
without letting go of hope.

I can't fix it all.
I can't carry every cry.
But I can keep my eyes open—
I can *see*,
and *pray*,
and *stand*,
and *love*.

Even when it's heavy.
Even when it's too much.
Even when the world turns away.

Because You are still watching.
Still waiting.
Still working.

And I want to be found
with my eyes wide open.

Scripture Reference
Matthew 9:36 (NIV)

*"When he saw the crowds, he had compassion on them,
because they were harassed and helpless,
like sheep without a shepherd."*

Until the Trumpet Sounds

A Poetic Prayer of Holy Readiness

I walk this world with eyes upturned,
A pilgrim on a road of dust.
I build, I bless, I break, I mend—
But never place my full-born trust.

For something stirs beneath the wind,
A sound not heard, but deeply known—
A whisper carried through the years,
A call to bring the wanderers home.

I do not know the hour, Lord,
Nor how the heavens will be split—
But still I live like it is near,
And let my soul stay candle-lit.

I'll love with urgency and grace,
I'll serve as if the time is short—
For every kindness is a seed
That testifies in Heaven's court.

I'll keep my hands upon the plow,
My heart awake, my spirit sound—
And run this race until the day
I hear that final trumpet sound.

And when it comes, I won't look back—
No fear, no shame, no earthly claim.
For all I've done, I've done for You—
And You alone will speak my name.

So keep me faithful, keep me clean,
Keep oil burning in my flame—
Until I rise to meet the One
Who knows and calls me just the same.

Scripture Reference
1 Thessalonians 4:16–17 (NIV)

"For the Lord himself will come down from heaven,
with a loud command, with the voice of the archangel
and with the trumpet call of God…
And so we will be with the Lord forever."

The Edge of the Hour

A Poetic Prayer of Final Watchfulness

Lord,
I feel it.

Like a string pulled tight
at the edge of sound.
Like the hush
before the hammer falls.
Like breath drawn in
but not yet released.

This is the edge of the hour.

The light feels thinner.
The shadows speak louder.
Even time seems to tremble
as it ticks.

You said we wouldn't know the moment.
You said to stay ready.
And here I am—
heart awake,
spirit still,
lamp lit.

I'm not looking for signs.
I'm listening
for **You**.

For the sound of justice
riding on the wind.
For the final mercy
wrapped in trumpet fire.
For the breath of Heaven
breaking through the veil.

Don't let me fall asleep here.
Don't let my oil run dry.
Let me be one of the few
who watched long
and didn't waver.

Because when the edge becomes eternity—
when the hour becomes the flame—
I want to be found *still believing*.
Still waiting.
Still Yours.

Scripture Reference
Mark 13:35–37 (NIV)

"Therefore keep watch because you do not know when the owner of the house will come back...
If he comes suddenly, do not let him find you sleeping."

I Still Believe He's Coming

A Poetic Prayer of Enduring Hope

Lord,
They say it's been too long.
That the sky's been silent,
That the stars don't speak,
That maybe You were never coming at all.

But I remember what You said.
And even if every calendar fades,
Even if generations pass into dust,
Even if the waiting breaks my bones—

I still believe.

I still believe You're coming—
not as a whisper this time,
but as thunder.
Not in a manger,
but in majesty.

I believe the sky will split.
That knees will bow—willing or not.
That justice will ride with mercy
and truth will stand unshaken.

I believe because the ache in me
isn't just hope—
it's memory.
Like something inside me
already knows
what it's waiting for.

So I'll watch the horizon.
I'll scan the wind.
I'll live today like it could be
the last sunrise before the shout.

They can laugh.
They can doubt.
They can sleep.

But as for me—
I'll keep my soul awake,
my lamp burning,
and my eyes on the eastern sky.

Because I still believe You're coming.
And I want to be the first to say—
"Welcome back."

Scripture Reference
2 Peter 3:3–4, 8–9 (NIV)
"In the last days scoffers will come... saying, 'Where is this 'coming' he promised?'...
But do not forget this one thing, dear friends... With the Lord a day is like a thousand years...
The Lord is not slow in keeping his promise..."

I Am Still the Watchman

A Poetic Prayer of Unshaken Vigilance

Lord,
The wall is quiet now.
Most have gone back to sleep,
their lamps cold,
their hearts content to wait
without watching.

But I am still here.
Still scanning the shadows.
Still listening for the tremble
of Heaven's footfall.

Not because I'm stronger,
but because You asked me to stay.

I am still the watchman.

Still holding the line
when it's easier to wander.
Still sounding the cry
when the hour grows late.
Still believing
that the King is coming
even if the road remains empty for a while.

My eyes are tired.
My shoulders ache.
But I have oil.
And I have hope.

And I will not leave my post.

Because You stood for me
when I was asleep in sin.
You kept watch
when I didn't even know I needed keeping.

So now I keep it in return.

Not for applause.
Not for reward.
But for love.

So let them scoff.
Let them sleep.
Let the wind howl if it must.

I will be on this wall
when the trumpet sounds.
When the sky splits.
When glory floods the world like dawn.

And I'll be ready to cry out—
**"He is here.
I saw Him coming."**

Scripture Reference
Isaiah 62:6 (NIV)
"I have posted watchmen on your walls, Jerusalem;
they will never be silent day or night..."

Section IV: The Last Sunrise

The return. The rising. The glory we've waited for.

The sky begins to burn with light.
Not destruction—**deliverance**.
These are the songs we saved for the final hour.
For the morning when graves break open,
when names are called,
when all that was promised
becomes all that we see.
This is the sunrise we've been singing toward.

Don't Close Your Eyes

A Poetic Prayer to the Weary and Waiting

Lord,
I feel the weariness in the air—
heavy,
quiet,
settling in like fog on a soul
that's been waiting too long.

I see it in the eyes
of the ones who once burned bright—
now flickering,
now fading,
now so close to letting go.

So this is my prayer—
to them.
To me.
To anyone still reaching
with trembling hands:

Don't close your eyes.

Not yet.
Not now.
Not when the sky is just about to crack
with light.

Don't let the waiting steal your watchfulness.
Don't let the silence convince you He's not coming.
Don't trade your oil
for comfort.
Don't trade your faith
for sleep.

Because He is nearer than we know.
The air is humming with eternity.
The shadows are thinning.

And grace is moving like dawn
through the bones of the world.

So stay awake.
Even if your eyelids tremble.
Even if your hope is a whisper.

Keep your heart lit.
Keep your soul ready.
Keep your hands open.

He's almost here.
And when He comes—
when the last sunrise shatters the sky—
you'll want to be found
still watching.
Still burning.
Still believing.

Don't close your eyes.
The light is almost here.

Scripture Reference
Romans 13:11 (NIV)
"The hour has already come for you to wake up from your slumber,
because our salvation is nearer now than when we first believed."

The Sky Will Split

A Poetic Prayer of the King's Return

Lord,
I don't know what it will look like—
only that it will be
more.

More than trumpets.
More than thunder.
More than anything I've ever dared
to imagine in the quiet
when no one was watching me pray.

But I believe
the sky will split.

Not gently.
Not politely.
But like glory can't be held back anymore.

Like Heaven's floodgates
have grown heavy
with centuries of mercy
and You've finally said,
"Now."

The clouds will peel like pages,
the light will burn like truth,
and every eye will see
what we were made for.

No more doubting.
No more hiding.
No more delay.

Just the King—
riding on radiance,
robed in righteousness,

eyes like fire
and a voice like rushing waters.

And in that moment,
I don't want to run.
I don't want to hide.
I don't want to wish
I had done more,
prayed more,
loved more.

So prepare me, Lord.
Let me live with that sky in my spirit.
Let me walk with that moment
pressed into my every step.

Because when the sky splits—
I want to be found
on my feet,
eyes open,
heart surrendered,
whispering…

**"He came.
Just like He said."**

Scripture Reference
Revelation 19:11 (NIV)

*"I saw heaven standing open and there before me was a white horse,
whose rider is called Faithful and True…"*

The First Light of Forever

A Poetic Prayer of Eternal Arrival

Lord,
I don't know what my first step
into forever will feel like—
but I know it will be light.

Not just sunlight—
but *You-light.*
Light that doesn't just shine—
it heals.

I imagine silence first.
Not the empty kind,
but the holy hush
of everything being
right.

The weight gone.
The ache gone.
The shame that clung like smoke—
lifted in a breath.

And then…
the face.

Yours.

No veil.
No metaphor.
Just the King
in full mercy,
full majesty,
and somehow still
the same Shepherd
who called me by name
when I was lost in the dark.

And in that moment,
I won't ask a single question.
I won't explain.
I won't perform.

I'll just fall.
Or rise.
Or both.

And whisper what my soul
has rehearsed since it first believed:

"This is what I was made for."

So until that first light—
I'll walk in shadows.
I'll bear the ache.
I'll keep the lamp burning
for the sunrise that never sets.

Because I know it's coming.
And when it does—
I'll be home.

Scripture Reference
1 Corinthians 13:12 (NIV)

*"Now we see only a reflection as in a mirror;
then we shall see face to face."*

When My Name Is Called

A Poetic Prayer of Divine Recognition

Lord,
I've answered to many names in this life—
some true,
some twisted,
some I picked up just to survive.

Failure.
Fighter.
Forgotten.
Faithful.

But none of them
sound the way I imagine
my name on Your lips.

Because when You say it—
everything else will fall away.

No accusation will follow.
No shame will cling.
No wound will whisper louder than
Your welcome.

And I'll know, in that single breath,
that I was always seen.
Always known.
Always loved.

I won't need a scroll.
I won't need a speech.
I'll just step forward
when Heaven speaks
the name You gave me
before the stars were born.

And in that sound,
I'll find my home.
My healing.
My whole.

So teach me to walk
as one already chosen.
To live like my name
is written where moth cannot touch
and time cannot fade.

Because one day soon—
the trumpet will shout,
the heavens will part,
and You will speak…

and I will answer.

Scripture Reference
Revelation 3:5 (NIV)

"I will never blot out the name of that person from the book of life, but will acknowledge that name before my Father and his angels."

Let the Last Light Be Love

A Poetic Prayer of Eternal Surrender

Lord,
When it's all said and done—
when the skies fall quiet
and the final sunrise stretches across forever—
let the last light be **love**.

Not wrath.
Not thunder.
Not even glory that blinds.

Let it be love that finds me.

The same love that stitched the stars
into the fabric of night.
The same love that wept at tombs
and bled at the edge of a hill.
The love that whispered over my ashes
and never walked away.

I don't want to meet You
with clenched fists
or shaking fear.

I want to meet You
with open hands.
With the heart of a child
who sees their Father's face
and runs—not because they must,
but because they *can*.

Let the last light be soft—
not weak,
but **welcoming**.

Let it wrap around the weary.
Let it draw in the doubting.

Let it hold the broken
like the arms I've dreamed of
when the world felt cold.

I don't need streets of gold
if You are there.
I don't need crowns
if I can fall at Your feet.

Just let it be love
that calls my name.
Let it be love
that lifts my face.
Let it be love
that fills the sky
and says—

"You made it home."

Scripture Reference
1 John 4:16 (NIV)

"God is love. Whoever lives in love lives in God, and God in them."

The Morning We Rise

A Poetic Prayer of Resurrection and Restoration

Lord,
I've buried many things.
Dreams.
Years.
Pieces of myself I thought would never breathe again.

I've stood beside graves—
some in the earth,
some in my spirit—
and whispered, *"Is this the end?"*

But You've always had
one more sunrise in Your hands.

So I believe in the morning.
Not just any morning—
but **the morning we rise.**

When the ground gives back what it never owned.
When every tomb is silenced.
When bones remember how to dance.
When sorrow sighs its last and joy begins to sing.

The morning when every scar is a story,
not a wound.
The morning when the body
and the soul
are whole again.

We will rise—
not in fear,
but in fire.
Not in doubt,
but in **divine design.**

We will rise because You did.
Because the grave wasn't strong enough
to keep You quiet—
and now it can't keep us either.

So I live for that day.
I wait for that light.
And when it comes,
I'll be ready.

Not perfect.
But promised.

Not whole.
But *His*.

Scripture Reference
Romans 6:5 (NIV)

*"For if we have been united with him in a death like his,
we will certainly also be united with him in a resurrection like his."*

All Things New

A Poetic Prayer of Eternal Renewal

Lord,
You are not in the business
of touching things up.
You are the God
who makes all things **new**.

Not patched.
Not polished.
Not painted over.

New.

And one day—
when the last tear falls,
when the trumpet's echo fades,
when dust and breath reunite
under eternal skies—

You'll speak again.

The same voice
that said, *"Let there be light,"*
will say, *"Behold—"*
and we'll see it with our own eyes.

The curse reversed.
The weight lifted.
The ache gone.

And every piece of this broken world
will bow to beauty.

No more night.
No more grave.
No more war between what is and what should be.

Just **You.**

And us,
restored.
Refined.
Reborn.

Until then,
teach me to live like it's coming.
To build like it matters.
To walk in the ruins
with resurrection in my bones.

Because I believe—
not just in Heaven,
but in *You.*

The One who said:
"I am making all things new."
And meant every word.

Scripture Reference
Revelation 21:5 (NIV)

*"He who was seated on the throne said,
'I am making everything new!'"*

Closing Prayer – "Until the Dawn"

Lord,
If these pages have reached anyone,
let it be because **You were in them**.

If these words stirred a soul,
let it lead them closer to the One who never stopped watching.

We have sung through the night,
through the ash,
through the waiting.

And now we lift our faces toward the sky
in hope,
in stillness,
in joy.

May our lamps stay lit.
May our hearts stay open.

And may we be found
singing—
until the dawn.

Amen.

About the Author

Tod Truettner is a builder by trade, a poet by calling, and a man whose journey has been forged in both fire and faith. With hands shaped for steel and wood, and a heart shaped by loss, love, and redemption, Tod writes not from theory—but from experience.

He knows what it means to stand in the dark and wait for the light.
He's battled illness, grief, and silence.
He's known the ache of watching loved ones leave this world, and the glory of walking with those still here.

But above all, Tod has learned this:
Grace endures.
Hope rises.
And love—the kind that stands guard through the night—*never lets go*.

His writing is raw, reverent, and real—meant not to impress, but to heal.
He writes for the weary, the willing, and the ones still whispering prayers through cracked voices.

Tod lives his faith out loud.
Through poetry.
Through pain.
Through the quiet moments where the soul meets the Savior in sacred surrender.

Songs for the Last Sunrise is his second book—a continuation of the story only God could write, and Tod was faithful enough to speak.